The Parable Quest

By Rick Overholtzer

Creative Force Press

The Parable Quest
© 2017 by Rick Overholtzer

This title is also available as an eBook. Visit www.CreativeForcePress.com/titles for more information.

Published by Creative Force Press
4704 Pacific Ave, Suite C, Lacey, WA 98503
www.CreativeForcePress.com

All rights reserved. No part of this publication may be reproduced, stored in a retrieval system, or transmitted in any form or by any means--for example, electronic, photocopy, recording--without the prior written permission of the publisher.

THE HOLY BIBLE, NEW INTERNATIONAL VERSION®, NIV®
Copyright © 1973, 1978, 1984, 2011 by Biblica, Inc.®
Used by permission. All rights reserved worldwide.

ISBN: 978-1-939989-27-7

Interior art by Bill Simpson

Printed in the United States of America

Dedication

A special thank you goes to my Lord and Savior, Jesus Christ, who I hope this book will honor.

To my wife and best friend for her encouraging me.

To my friends who have read it and given me their input.

To Douglas Pankretz for his hard work at putting it all together and his encouragement.

And to you the reader, for without you this would not be possible.

Contents

Introduction	7
1 David Broz's Parable Quest Remembrance	11
2 Gabe Smith's Parable Quest Remembrance	55
3 Brother John's Parable Quest Remembrance	65
4 The Heart of Praise	87
5 Eulogy	95
6 Background of Pastor Rich by Mrs. Norton	107
Discussion Guide	115
About the Author	121

Introduction

Pastor Rich Norton was my youth pastor, a wonderful teacher and friend. Now he was lying in a hospital bed with what the doctor's say was a massive heart attack. Even though my full name is Jonathan, Pastor Rich always called me Jon.

I really did not know what to expect, considering it had been a few years since I had seen him. Even worse, I didn't want to remember him with a network of tubes and wires plugged into him, but I pushed that all aside and remembered why I was there. Not for my sake, but for his, praying God would use me to bless him even as he lay dying.

Quietly I stepped into his room, not wanting to disturb him. Jennifer, his wife, was there by his side and began to weep when she saw me. I walked up to his bed, he opened his eyes slowly, and recognized me. "Jon, come close please," Pastor Rich said. "Do you remember the Parable Quest?"

"Yes I do," I said with confidence, even though my mind furiously searched my memories, trying to recall what it all meant. Ah yes, a spark of something was found in my mind's archives. "You told us stories that you made up about Jesus Christ's parables from the Bible."

His eyes sparkled as I began to share a little of what I remembered.

Then the most unexpected thing happened. Pastor Rich sat up with a determined effort and said to me, "You have to find out, Jon, if the others remember it also. And put the stories into a book, please!" Rich laid back down and closed his eyes again to rest.

Jennifer came over to me and gave me a big hug. Then the nurse came in and told me it was time for his medication and other things and asked if I might step out of the room.

Now what am I going to do? I thought.

Chapter 1

David Broz's Parable Quest Remembrance

My pastor's dying wish was for me to find the other four boys who were in his Sunday School class in a very small community nearly eight years ago and gather whatever they remember of his stories. I estimated we were all between the ages of 26-30 now. *Who knows where they all are now,* I wondered, *but I know where to start my search.*

When I got home I surfed the Internet and found one family who still lived in the same area. I dialed the number and a pleasant older woman answered the phone.

"Is this Mrs. Broz?"

She responded shyly, "Yes it is."

I told her I was a friend of Rich Norton who was

the former youth pastor at their church and explained my recent visit with him in the hospital.

"Is Pastor Rich okay?" she asked, alarmed.

"He had a massive heart attack and he really could use your prayers. I need to know if your son, David attended his class."

"Why, yes he did," she replied.

"Is there any way I can contact your son?" I gently asked.

She gave me his e-mail and said that it's the best way to communicate with him.

"Thank you, Mrs. Broz," I replied. "Pastor Rich is at Mason General Hospital if you would like to contact him."

This is great, a solid lead, I thought while running upstairs to my computer. A sense of excitement came over me as I set up a new e-mail account called Parable Quest and began my anonymous e-mail to David:

"Hi, I am a friend of Pastor Rich and I have been asked to contact those students who attended his class when he shared the Parable Quest stories. I am requesting any memories or stories that you can share with me to put into a book as a presentation and preservation for Pastor Rich. I am also looking for Gabe and John Smith, and Bill Simpson, so if you happen to know how I could contact them, let me know."

I hit SEND on my email, accompanied by a prayer.

The weekend was here and I looked forward to a relaxing, warm September day. I phoned the hospital to see how Pastor Rich was doing. The news was not good.

After the hospital update, I checked my e-mail and found the usual spam, and in with them was a message from Mrs. David Broz, which read:

"David is away on a business trip, but this is his wife. He had been on a mission trip a couple years ago and was interviewed afterwards. His interview was printed in a Missions periodical. He talks about the Parable Quest in it, so I hope this helps." (See Attached File)

When I clicked the file attachment, this story documented the events of his trip:

The night was cool and crisp in the farthest part of South America. A small group of six missionaries had boarded a plane in Los Angeles to bring Bibles to an un-churched region.

Now, after 36 hours, two planes, three airports, a bus, and an open jeep they found themselves on a narrow road at the edge of a thick jungle.

Included in the missionary group was David, fresh out of college, and Tom in his 50's, a new pastor to the church. They were both picked by prayer to venture out with a local guide named Najui.

The rest of the team set up camp with the local pastor.

David and Tom got busy unloading the vehicles and sorted out their packs for the long hike ahead.

Najui was 19 years old, tall and thin with a contagious smile. He spoke very good English. When asked about it, he replied that many years ago English settlers came and many in his village learned English. He shared that the leadership of the country was hostile to Christians, so the three of them would have to smuggle in the Bibles.

David and Tom hiked along carrying their cargo to a remote village. Najui walked ahead, scouting the rough dirt road they traveled. Tom fell in stride beside young David and asked him, "David, how did you become a Christian?"

David considered the question and then began, "My parents took me to church at an early age, and they told me about Jesus. At eleven years old I remember asking Jesus in my heart."

David tripped a little from a root in the road, then continued, "I went to Sunday School every week and listened to the Bible stories, and I had this one really memorable teacher who told us a series of stories he called the Parable Quest."

"Sounds like a creative teacher," Tom responded. "What was the Parable Quest?"

"It was the parables Jesus taught, and the Sunday School teacher used them in his stories," David replied.

Up ahead, Najui stopped abruptly, turned and motioned silently for them to hide themselves and their contraband cargo beside the road in the dense brush.

From behind the enormous leaves of a tropical shrub, David watched as five men carrying rifles appeared from around the bend and walked toward them. David closed his eyes and prayed silently, "Jesus protect us and make us unseen by these men."

The sound of boots on gravel grew faint and David opened his eyes, peering up and down the road with his pastor, but neither of them saw the armed men. They seemed to have disappeared. "Praise God!" he exclaimed within himself.

Najui looked at him puzzled and said, "Men came but they turned and ran away without even looking."

"We must take hands and pray for our safety so that we can fulfill this mission, and that God will continue to protect us," Tom urged.

They prayed and Najui said, "Follow the road for seven miles, then we will follow the trail that will take us the back way to my village. Once we reach the trail, we can go to the shelter I have made and rest for a while."

The sky was beautiful blue and clear, with just hints of clouds.

The road was easy to follow because it was open,

but the lack of cover also made it very dangerous for them.

David and Tom carried the crates stacked together with rope handles on each side. They had gloves, but the weight and size of these crates made it impossible to travel too far without stopping to rest. Najui was always on the lookout and continued ahead of them, and then would come back to see how they were doing.

During one instance when Najui was out ahead of them, David felt a chill go down his back and fear struck. David looked at Tom and pointed to the brush beside them. Moving quickly with the crates, they hid themselves the best they could as two strangers walked swiftly past.

David's thoughts quickly turned to Najui as he prayed, "Dear Jesus protect Najui."

The two men came back by, but this time there were three of them. To their horror the third one was Najui standing between the two men as they walked. Tom heard Najui call out in English, "Don't worry I'll be back soon. Stay put!"

Tom and David prayed again for their safety and Najui, then they moved to a small clearing behind the bushes where they could hide. Leaving the crates in the bushes Tom whispered, "Tell me more about the Parable Quest."

David started from the beginning.

The Parable Quest begins with two young men named Jakabee and Gunther who came from a small village in Germany named Overhous. They had been commissioned by the townspeople to go and share the Good News that Jesus Christ had risen. With just five Bibles, two small sabers, a compass, and some matches, they began their adventure.

They traveled by a small, cutout wooden boat down a tranquil river.

Stepping off onto the shore and tying up the

boat, they found themselves in the Northwest Territories called Googlestein. They knew they must get beyond the cliffs in order to reach the villages.

Jakabee watched an eagle fly overhead, and then navigate through the thick brush towards a small trail that led between the crags. They followed the eagle until they reached an opening through the cliff.

Jakabee first entered through the small opening, then Gunther followed. But just as Gunther stepped through he lost his footing and fell forward, pushing Jakabee downhill.

Falling, they both tumbled down the steep, dirty ravine. As they skidded to the bottom of the ravine, they landed on shrubby bushes that cushioned their fall.

"Boo!" Najui bellowed, startling David and Tom, ending the budding story.

Najui began to laugh as Tom and David recovered from their fright.

They grilled Najui about what had happened with the two men. "They were looking for us, but they now are looking in a completely different area from here," explained Najui. "If they caught you, you would be dead right now, but praise God they do not know English and God saved us again."

"The Parable Quest will wait," David said. "We must get these crates to the village before we are found out."

Tom agreed.

Lifting up the crates they started their long trek again. Walking was grueling, and just about the time they were ready to stop, Najui said, "It's just on up ahead, not much farther, and we can rest for a while."

David knew Najui said just on up ahead, but it seemed as if they walked another 40 minutes before they finally arrived at their destination. The shelter was meager: just poles between two trees with a dark-colored canvas thrown over it. They relaxed for a bit, hiding the crates beneath branches and behind thick brush.

After what seemed like a momentary rest, Najui was up and ready for them to move on. "It will be dark soon. We must keep going." They started again by praying together.

David felt a little ashamed, because his prayer requests had only been about their safety and not for the people they were there to bless. Tom finished his prayer for the villagers and for strength to fulfill their expedition. Then Najui provided some food for them to eat, and it tasted surprisingly good.

The trail was not at all what David pictured as a proper trail. In his estimation, a trail was something where two or more people could easily pass one other on and should be easily recognizable as a trail.

This was certainly not that. They were walking over brush and logs and maneuvering around rocks and trees, but they were confident Najui knew where he was going.

"I hear voices," whispered Tom. They stood still as they heard several people coming closer down the trail.

Hiding themselves behind some brush with the crates between Tom and David, they waited to see who it was. *Isn't this Najui's hidden trail that supposedly only he knows about*, David wondered, as four young boys went scurrying past them.

Najui leapt to his feet and began calling to the boys.

Tom and David's hearts sank, and they stared at one another in fear.

Najui smiled as he said, "These are my brothers." The four boys came to them and took the crates of Bibles, for which Tom and David were eternally thankful.

The boys led the way with the crates, and when the group entered the village the townspeople gathered around the crates.

Najui smiled as he spoke to the people in his language.

The crates were carefully opened as if there was something very fragile in them, and once opened, the towns people cheered. The village had no more than about 50 people, but the joy on their faces made David all the more grateful to God for allowing them to experience this moment.

Each person, young and old, came forward, and Najui handed them their very own Bible. Their joy was unmistakable.

It reminded David of when his parents gave him his first Bible and the happiness it gave him.

When they finished, Najui showed them the hut

they would be staying in.

"Rest my friends, because there will be a great feast tonight," Najui said.

Tom and David went inside their hut which was much nicer than the makeshift jungle shelter. There was a table and two chairs with two well-made cots for them to sleep on. The walls were decorated with colorful drawings which reminded David of impressionist art like Monet's.

Tom told David he had to hear more of the Parable Quest or he wouldn't be able to go to sleep. By this time David had forgotten where he had left off, but not Tom. "It was when they fell on some brush that cushioned their fall," Tom said.

David began again where he had left off.

A group of birds began to attack them as they got to their feet. A nest had been disturbed. Thrashing around with their sabers and looking for a way of escape, they ran over a mound of large rocks that revealed thorn bushes on the other side. Once they reached the thorn bushes the birds gave up the attack. Now they had to cut through the thorn bushes to get out of the area.

The sharp thorns grabbed their clothing and scratched exposed skin, so Jakabee and Gunther moved slowly and cautiously through the underbrush, eventually reaching a lush green lawn with an apple grove.

Each step was like walking on green velvet and the red apples were delicious. They leaned against one of the trees and Jakabee pulled out his Bible and read, "Jesus spoke in many parables, saying; 'A farmer went out to sow his seed. As he was scattering the seed, some fell along the path, and birds came and ate it up. Some fell on rocky places, where it did not have much soil. It sprang up quickly, because the soil was shallow. But when the sun came up, the plants were scorched, and they withered because they had no root.

Other seed fell among thorns, which grew up and choked the plants. Still other seed fell on good soil, where it produced a crop-a hundred, sixty or thirty times what was sown. He who has ears, let him hear. Listen then to what the parable of the sower means: When anyone hears the message about the kingdom and does not understand it, the evil one comes and snatches away what was sown in his heart. This is the seed sown along the path.

The one who received the seed that fell on rocky places is the man who hears the word, and at once, receives it with joy. But since he has no root, he lasts only a short time.

When trouble or persecution comes because of the word, he quickly falls away.

The one who received the seed that fell among the thorns is the man who hears the word, but the worries of this life and the deceitfulness of wealth chokes it, making it unfruitful.

But the one who received the seed that fell on good soil is the man who hears the word and understands it. He produces a crop, yielding a hundred, sixty or thirty times what was sown."

Jakabee said, "Wow! We just experienced this parable by the birds, thorns, scorching sun and then the fruitful trees. God make us fruitful," he prayed.

Jakabee and Gunther were exhausted and they slept peacefully as the Lord gave them rest.

They awoke to encouragement from the Holy Spirit to go to the people who were on ahead. The apple orchard was vast, but they soon found a convenient dirt road, easy to travel on. As they walked, Jakabee noticed two wooden homes being built along the road: one with an immense foundation with a modest home on it, and next to it was a lavishly built, multi-level home, which seemed to have little or no foundation whatsoever.

This lavish house had beautiful windows that sparkled as the sun hit them. The windows were so large that the view from the inside would most certainly be marvelous. The only thing that out-shined the windows was the bright red front doors with shimmering gold hardware.

From there they traveled a considerable distance up a hill, winding upward on the switchbacks. At the top, they looked out over from where they had come and watched as the wind move through the valley. The tempest arose and swept across the two homes. The beautiful home toppled to the ground with a mighty crash, shaking the earth beneath it.

Jakabee was troubled at the devastation. Gunther put his hand on his shoulder and reminded him of what Jesus Christ had said, "I will show you what he is like who comes to Me and hears My words and puts them into practice. He is like a man building a house who dug down deep and laid the foundation on rock. When a flood came the torrent struck that house, but could not shake it, because it was well built. But the one who hears My words and does not put them into practice is like a man who built a house on the ground without a foundation, the moment the torrent struck that house, it collapsed and its destruction was complete."

They ran down the hill and came to the heap of rubble. Finding that no one was inside, they talked about their need to know and follow God's Word more carefully.

"Silence!" Najui interrupted the story. "Get rested and ready for tonight."

So, David laid back on his cot and fell asleep. "Celebrate Jesus, Celebrate, Celebrate Jesus, Celebrate." David heard himself singing in a dream, and the music was heavenly.

David awoke to Tom's off-key voice singing to

some music. That alone would wake anyone up, but David didn't tell Tom about his sour notes. Tom seemed so excited, and David didn't want to offend him. Since God only requires a joyful noise, who was he to object?

Having only napped a few hours, they were a little groggy when they awoke. It was evening as they came out of the tent, and they saw all the villagers rejoicing before the Lord. The presence of the Holy Spirit filled the village, and the sights and sounds were wonderful – even beyond expression.

David knelt on the ground and lifted up his hand and began to sing in an unknown language as the Spirit led. He cried, "Holy, Holy is the Lord God Almighty, Who was and is to come. Praise be to Your name Jesus, and let Your Name be magnified."

Tom was nowhere to be seen until David ventured to where some villagers were dancing. Shocked to see old Tom out there dancing before the Lord, and doing a mighty fine job of it, he waved his greetings.

God is incredibly wonderful to allow them this experience, David thought, *and to enjoy His presence and feel His love.* Just when they thought it couldn't get any better, the celebration slowed, as a deep reverence came over everyone and they stood in awe of the magnificent God.

Preparing for the meal that the whole village had arranged, each person began to sit around the large makeshift tables. It was like a potluck back home when everyone brought some food to share and there was always more than enough. This food was very strange to them, but David ate it just the same and it all tasted fantastic. Time had no meaning when this celebration was going on.

David noticed the sun was starting to come up as everyone finished eating.

He couldn't grasp what he was seeing. *Wait, I'm lost – has this feast lasted all evening and throughout the night? How can it be morning already?*

Exhausted, the villagers started putting things away as one by one they returned to their huts for a daybreak rest.

Tom and David had been one of the last to retire because of their late afternoon nap the day before, yet by the time they reached their cots they both crashed into a deep sleep.

"Leave quickly, danger, danger!" They were awakened by Najui coming into their room screaming.

David jumped up as Tom reached for his pack, and they went out into the bright light of the noon day sun which made them both wince as their eyes adjusted. Najui grabbed David's hand as he led them toward the trail they previously had taken.

"Run as fast as you can," Najui insisted, my young brothers are already on the trail waiting to help you. "Go quickly!" he shouted.

David being younger than Tom had no problem sprinting, but David soon found himself waiting while Tom caught up. David took his pack from him. That helped lighten Tom's load and slowed David down a bit.

Over one fallen tree, down a small embankment, through some heavy brush and there was one of Najui's brothers who waved them to follow. One of the other brothers came to help with the pack and led them to the shelter Najui had built, where they had stayed the day before.

One of the four brothers said, "Wait Najui, wait Najui," and he pointed to the shelter.

Panting heavily Tom said, "We need to pray."

Just as he began to pray, "Boo!" Najui startled them again as he came up behind.

David nearly knocked over one of the shelter's poles as Tom began to laugh and then they all laughed.

"What happened back there?" David insisted, as he regained his composure.

Najui shared with them the events that led to their departure. "Remember the two men from the road who I led away? I saw them in our village and they directed their attention to you both, and were pointing to your hut. They walked away, so I had you leave quickly to keep from getting caught.

"What I did not know," Najui continued, "was that these men had come last night during the celebration and found themselves caught up in the Holy Spirit of God.

"They talked with one of our elders, who led them in prayer of salvation by confessing their sins, and asking Jesus to be their Lord and Savior. These two men joined in the celebration as new believers, but I did not see them until this morning. We have time if you want to come back and meet them or you can continue on to meet up with your other missionaries."

Tom thought that since they had come this far, it would be best to continue on to their other missionary party. David agreed.

Najui smiled and said, "Jesus has protected you this whole way, and I pray for your continual protection as you travel back." Najui and his brothers gathered around them and put their hands on their shoulders and prayed.

David closed his eyes as they prayed, and when he opened them Najui and his brothers were gone. David and Tom were shocked that they were gone so quickly.

Resting at the shelter, Tom smiled and said, "Finish what happened to Jakabee and Gunther after the tempest."

"Okay, okay," said David:

As Jakabee and Gunther continued walking, dusk settled in as a greenish-yellow glow over a city that lay ahead. Gunther had a Scripture come to mind about being ready to give an account of their faith, the faith in the Only Begotten Son of God (Jesus), and the Good News of Salvation to those who believe.

Jesus shared, "The harvest is plentiful, but the workers are few. Ask the Lord of the harvest, therefore, to send out workers into His field. Go! I am sending you out like lambs among wolves. Do not take a purse or bag or sandals, and do not greet anyone on the road. When you enter a house first say, 'Peace to this house.'

If a man of peace is there, your peace will rest on him; if not, it will return to you. Stay in that house, eating and drinking whatever they give you, for the worker deserves his wages.

Do not move around from house to house.

When you enter a town and are welcomed, eat what is set before you. Heal the sick who are there and tell them, 'The Kingdom of God is near you.' But when you enter a town and are not welcomed, go into its streets and say, 'Even the dust of your town that sticks to our feet we wipe off against you.' Yet be sure of this, 'The Kingdom of God is near.'"

Jakabee's heart ached for the people of the city up ahead. Jakabee prayed, "Lord, I ask that the Holy Spirit go ahead of us to prepare the hearts of these people from the youngest to the oldest, and let Your light of salvation touch their unbelieving hearts, Amen."

Gunther began reading out of his Bible, "Suppose one of you has a hundred sheep and loses one of them? Does he not leave the ninety-nine in the open country and go after the lost sheep until he finds it? And when he finds it, he joyfully puts it on his shoulders and goes home. Then he calls his friends and neighbors together and says, 'Rejoice with me, I have found my lost sheep.'

Jesus said, 'I tell you this, the same way there will be more rejoicing in heaven over one sinner who repents than over ninety-nine righteous persons who do not need to repent.

Or suppose a woman has ten silver coins and loses one. Does she not light a lamp, sweep the house and search carefully until she finds it? And when she finds it, she calls her friends and neighbors together and says, 'Rejoice with me; I have found my lost coin.'

'In the same way,' Jesus said, 'there is rejoicing in the presence of the angels of God over one sinner who repents.'"

Jakabee and Gunther prayed for Jesus to forgive them of their sins and to cleanse them from all unrighteousness, also to give them boldness for the task at hand. Gunther told Jakabee they should go to the open field and pitch their tent, then go into the city in the morning. Gunther shared this parable from Jesus:

"A certain man was preparing a great banquet and invited many guests. At the time of the *banquet he sent his servant to tell those who had been invited, 'Come, for everything is now ready.'*

But they all alike began to make excuses. The first said, 'I have just bought a field, and I must go and see it. Please excuse me.' Another said, 'I have just bought five yoke of oxen, and I'm on my way to try them out. Please excuse me.' Still another said, 'I just got married, so I can't come.'

The servant came back and reported this to his master. Then the owner of the house became angry and ordered his servant, 'Go out quickly into the streets and alleys of the town and bring in the poor, the crippled, the blind and the lame.'

'Sir,' the servant said, 'what you ordered has been done, but there is still room.'

Then the master told his servant, 'Go out to the roads and country lanes and make them come in, so that my house will be full.

I tell you, not one of those men who were invited will get a taste of my banquet.'"

Gunther said to Jakabee, "We are the servants going out to invite those who will come to the banquet of our Lord." They both slept well until the brightness of the morning sun woke them, so they ate breakfast and trekked toward the city.

Tom stopped David and asked, "Do you know which way back to our team."

David smiled, I know the road is just up ahead and from there we can go south until we reach the team.

"My son has always called me Sir Lost-a-Lot," Tom said, "so I am glad I have someone with a good sense of direction."

The pair started on their journey back to the team

not more than six miles away.

Tom asked again, "Okay, keep going with the Parable Quest."

David picked up the story again.

Jakabee and Gunther were walking towards the city when a man in a blue robe appeared ahead of them. Jakabee thought he was a businessman by the suit that he wore. They tried to detain him, but he said he was in a rush, and he passed them.

Then another man approached in a long emerald green robe.

They tried to talk with him, too, but he waved on by, saying, "I'm too busy for this."

Yet another man appeared. This one looked like royalty by his jewels and fine clothing. He also passed with his head tilted up, "I will not socialize with commoners," he said.

Walking on they heard sounds of someone crying for help. Jakabee and Gunther turned to the side of the road and found a man beaten and left in the ditch. They picked him up and carried him until they reached the city.

They stopped a young boy who directed them to the doctor.

The doctor saw Jakabee and Gunther carrying the injured man and assisted them getting him into his office. The town was like an old western town with the big store fronts and signs, wooden walkways and horses tied up to railings. Several elderly men were sitting on the front porches watching everything go by.

Jakabee pondered over what had just happened and why the men on the road refused to take the time to help this poor man when help was needed.

Gunther shared another of Jesus' parables, "A man was going down from Jerusalem to Jericho when he fell into the hands of robbers. They stripped him of his clothes, beat him and went away, leaving him half dead. A priest happened to be going down the same road and when he saw the man, he passed by on the other side. So too, a Levite, when he came to the place and saw him, passed by on the other side.

But a Samaritan, as he traveled, came where the man was, and when he saw him, he took pity on him. He went to him and bandaged his wounds, pouring on oil and wine. Then he put the man on his own donkey, took him to an inn and took care of him.

The next day he took out two silver coins and gave them to the innkeeper. 'Look after him,' he said, 'and when I return, I will reimburse you for any extra expense you may have.'

'Which of these three do you think was a neighbor to the man who fell into the hands of robbers?' Jesus asked."

We were, thought Jakabee.

The love of God compelled them to minister to the lost wherever the Lord led.

Gunther read of the mustard seed and the lamp in the Bible. "The kingdom of heaven is like a mustard seed, which a man took and planted in his field. Though it is the smallest of all your seeds, yet when it grows, it is the largest of garden plants and becomes a tree, so that the birds of the air come and perch in its branches."

"No one lights a lamp and puts it in a place where it will be hidden, or under a bowl. Instead he puts it on its stand, so that those who come in may see the light. Your eye is the lamp of your body." Jakabee said, "Let us grow and glow so we can lead others to find rest in Jesus Christ as we have."

Gunther went to a street corner as Jakabee followed, and began looking up into the sky. Jakabee looked up but saw nothing, yet he was compelled to keep looking. Soon a crowd gathered, wondering what they were looking at.

Gunther saw the crowd and said, "Jesus Christ, my Lord and Savior, said He would return just as He was taken away. I stand here looking up to let you know that now is the time of salvation. The Bible says, 'If you confess with your mouth Jesus is Lord, and believe in your heart that God raised Him from the dead, you will be saved, and that there is salvation in no other.'"

Jakabee asked those who wanted forgiveness of sin and freedom to raise their hands. Almost all hands went up. Jakabee led them in a simple prayer, "God, I ask you to forgive me for the bad I have done and I ask Jesus Christ to be my Lord, and save me from all the wrongs I have committed. Amen."

Weeping, a man came forward and cried that his daughter was sick and asked if they would come and pray for her. They immediately left and went to the man's home, and found a young girl lying on a couch with fever.

Gunther went over to her and placed his hand on her head and prayed, then walked away and came back and prayed again. Five more times he did this. The girl smiled, for the fever had left. They all rejoiced. Jakabee left a Bible for them to share with other families.

The news spread of what God had done in their town, and many came for prayer and received Jesus Christ as their Lord and Savior. Jakabee and Gunther continued to minister to whomever came for healing or prayer.

Gunther explained that there was someone waiting for them in heaven with a white robe that says "King of kings and Lord of lords" on it, and Jesus is His name. At the name of Jesus every knee will bow and every tongue confess that He is Lord.

He will smile and call you by name, and put

His hand on your shoulder and say, "Well done good and faithful servant, enter into your rest."

Gunther divulged this parable, "When the Son of Man comes in His glory, and all the angels with Him, He will sit on His throne in heavenly glory, and all the nations will be gathered before Him. He will separate the people one from another as a shepherd separates the sheep from the goats. He will put the sheep on His right and the goats on His left.

Then the King will say to those on His right, 'Come, you who are blessed by My Father; take your inheritance, the kingdom prepared for you since the creation of the world. For I was hungry and you gave Me something to eat, I was thirsty and you gave Me something to drink, I was a stranger and you invited Me in. I needed clothes and you clothed Me, I was sick and you looked after Me, I was in prison and you came to visit Me.'

Then the righteous will answer him, 'Lord,

when did we see You hungry and feed You, or thirsty and give You something to drink? When did we see You a stranger and invite You in, or needing clothes and clothe You? When did we see You sick or in prison and go visit You?'

The King will reply, 'I tell you the truth, whatever you did for one of the least of these brothers of Mine, you did for Me.'

Then He will say to those on His left, 'Depart from Me, you who are cursed, into eternal fire prepared for the devil and his angels. For I was hungry and you gave Me nothing to eat, I was thirsty and you gave Me nothing to drink, I was a stranger and you did not invite Me in, I needed clothes and you did not clothe Me, I was sick and in prison and you did not look after Me.'

They also will answer, 'Lord, when did we see You hungry or thirsty or a stranger or needing clothes or sick or in prison, and did not help You?'

He will reply, 'I tell you the truth, whatever you did not do for one of the least of these, you did not do for Me.'

Then they will go away to eternal punishment, but the righteous to eternal life."

Tom yelled, "Look out!" as something in front of David fell from the tree. A large branch of a tree nearly fell on David. "A widow maker." Tom said.

"Thank God that He protected me again on our mission," David said. "Where are we on the Parable Quest?" he asked.

"We just finished the sheep and the goats," Tom replied.

"Tom have you seen how the Parable Quest has also been a part of our own quest?" remarked David.

"We have done what Jesus has asked us to and we are blessed for the experience of serving Him and blessed by the new friends we've made."

"Wow! You're right He has brought us through our own Parable Quest."

"Now, what's next in the story?" asked Tom.

David regained his thoughts.

Jakabee and Gunther stayed in the town for a time. They were never without someone giving them food and a place to stay while they were there, helping in exchange with repairs.

Jakabee instructed them from the Bible, "You are the salt of the earth. But if the salt loses its saltiness, how can it be made salty again? It is no longer good for anything, except to be thrown out and trampled by men. You are the light of the world, a city on a hill cannot be hidden. Neither do people light a lamp and put it under a bowl. Instead they put it on its stand, and it gives light to everyone in the house. In the same way, let your light so shine before men, that they may see your good deeds and praise your Father in heaven."

The last thing I can remember from my pastor's teaching was this final thought:

"Serving God is the greatest joy I could hope to do with my life. The Bible tells us to go and make disciples and to be ready in season and out of season to give an account of our faith that we have in Jesus Christ."

"That's all I remember, but there was so much more," said David.

Tom was stunned. "What a great story and what a great testimony of that Sunday School teacher!" Having walked a long time they were amazed at how gracious God had been to them. David sang a simple song that he had learned in Sunday School, "Jesus loves me this I know for the Bible tells me so, little ones to Him belong, they we are weak, but He is strong."

They saw the mission team they had left days ago on up ahead. Tom joined in and they started to sing all the louder until they reached the team. "Yes, Jesus loves me, yes, Jesus loves me, yes, Jesus loves me, the Bible tells me so."

Their mission team ran to them, and much rejoicing filled the air as they headed back home.

Along with this attached letter about her husband's South American mission trip experiences, Mrs. Broz finished off her e-mail by giving me Gabe Smith's email address. Gabe was one of the boys who David went to Sunday School with.

Jonathan turned off his computer and thanked God for this start of fulfilling the request of a dying man.

CHAPTER 2

Chapter 2

Gabe Smith's Parable Quest Remembrance

I e-mailed Gabe Smith anonymously with the same message I had sent to David. In response, Gabe sent me a reply with a link to this blog post he wrote:

After years of studying and hard work, I was finally getting my degree. *What have I worked so hard for? What can all this bring?* I thought to myself.

Getting a Master's degree is hard enough, but to have a Masters of Theology was something a person would have to have a calling for. I was raised by parents who did not appreciate my love and zeal for Jesus Christ. Oh they went to church, true, but Sunday was good enough to keep God happy.

"You don't have to read and study the Bible and all that religious stuff all the time," they would tell me.

I actually followed that line of thinking until I attended a Sunday School youth group. My teacher started a long running story called the Parable Quest. Rich Norton was my youth teacher who started these stories which I could not wait to hear every Sunday.

Pastor Rich was a master storyteller, because he would tell truths that inspired us, yet left us hanging with the story until the following week. I wondered how teacher Rich was doing after all these years, and does he know how much God used him to inspire me? I remembered that the youth classroom was small and musty. It was an older church, yet you could feel the Spirit of God there.

I remembered the musty smell of the boys youth room with the old chalk board and the six chairs. The carpet was a gold shag, but the chairs were new and had cushions on them. Thank God! Five boys, ages seven to sixteen, were in the class. The girls met in another room with Mrs. Butler.

I was one of the oldest and David was the youngest. My brother, John, and his best friend, Bill, attended the class as well. A boy named Jonathan was also there, but he was somewhat of the outcast since he seemed less interested in the Parable Quest than the rest of us. The room had windows with heavy glass and thick wood frames. Looking out you could only see the unattractive parking lot.

Here's what I remember of the Parable Quest.

Jakabee was younger and Gunther was the leader, as I remembered. While hiking above the shore with an eagle flying overhead, Jakabee and Gunther fell down a hill and landed on some briers. As they got up, they found they had landed beside a lush grassy field.

Gunther read from the Bible the Parable of the Sower.

I remember wanting to be the one sown on good soil, a person who understands God's Word and is fruitful in his life. That's the one I want to be, God.

In the story, Jakabee and Gunther journeyed to a land of people needing the truth of Christ. With their Bibles in hand they prepared their hearts to minister in prayer. As they began looking up to heaven many people gathered around them who also began looking up.

"Friends, I see you look to the sky yet there is nothing," said Gunther.

Gunther continued in the Bible, "Jesus Christ's disciples asked Him, 'Lord, are You at this time going to restore the kingdom to Israel?'

Jesus said, 'It is not for you to know the times or dates the Father has set by His own authority. But you will receive power when the Holy Spirit comes on you; and you will be my witnesses in Jerusalem, and in all Judea and Samaria, and to the ends of the earth.'

After He said this, He was taken up before their very eyes, and a cloud hid Him from their sight. They were looking intently up into the sky as He was going, when suddenly two men dressed in white stood beside them. 'Men of Galilee,' they said, 'why do you stand here looking into the sky? This same Jesus, Who has been taken from you into heaven, will come back in the same way you have seen Him go into heaven.'

Gunther continued, "We read in Revelation: 'Grace and peace to you from Him Who is, and

Who was, and Who is to come, and from the seven spirits before His throne, and from Jesus Christ, Who is the faithful witness, the firstborn from the dead, and the ruler of the kings of the earth. To Him who loves us and has freed us from our sins by His blood, and has made us to be a kingdom and priests to serve His God and Father—to Him be glory and power for ever and ever! Amen.

Look, He is coming with the clouds, and every eye will see Him, even those who pierced Him; and all the peoples of the earth will mourn because of Him. So shall it be! Amen. 'I am the Alpha and the Omega,' says the Lord God, 'Who is, and Who was, and Who is to come, the Almighty.'

"Hear this Parable," Gunther said, "of the sheep and their master":

"I tell you the truth, the man who does not enter the sheep pen by the gate, but climbs in by some other way, is a thief and a robber. The man who enters by the gate is the shepherd of his sheep. The watchman opens the gate for him, and the sheep listen to his voice.

He calls his own sheep by name and leads them out. When he has brought out all his own, he goes on ahead of them, and his sheep follow him because they know his voice. But they will never follow a stranger; in fact, they will run away from him because they do not recognize a stranger's voice."

"Jesus Christ used this figure of speech, but they did not understand what He was telling them. Therefore Jesus said again, 'I tell you the truth, I am the gate for the sheep. All who ever came before Me were thieves and robbers, but the sheep did not listen to them. I am the gate; whoever enters through Me will be saved. He will come in and go out, and find pasture."

The thief comes only to steal and kill and destroy; I have come that they may have life, and have it to the full.

I am the good shepherd. The good shepherd lays down His life for the sheep. The hired hand is not the shepherd who owns the sheep. So when he sees the wolf coming, he abandons the sheep and runs away. Then the wolf attacks the flock and scatters it.

The man runs away because he is a hired hand and cares nothing for the sheep. I am the good shepherd; I know my sheep and my sheep know Me— just as the Father knows Me and I know the Father—and I lay down My life for the sheep.

I have other sheep that are not of this sheep pen, and I must bring them also.

They too will listen to My voice, and there shall be one flock and one shepherd. The reason My Father loves Me is that I lay down My life— only to take it up again. No one takes it from Me, but I lay it down of My own accord. I have authority to lay it down and authority to take it up again. This command I received from my Father."

"God does not show favoritism, but accepts men from every nation who fear Him and do what is right. You know the message God sent to the people of Israel, telling the good news of peace through Jesus Christ, who is Lord of all.

You know what has happened throughout Judea, beginning in Galilee after the baptism that John preached—how God anointed Jesus of Nazareth with the Holy Spirit and power, and how He went around doing good and healing all who were under the power of the devil, because God was with Him.

We are witnesses of everything He did in the country of the Jews and in Jerusalem. They killed Him by hanging Him on a tree, but God raised Him from the dead on the third day and caused Him to be seen. He was not seen by all the people, but by witnesses whom God had already chosen—by us who ate and drank with Him after He rose from the dead.

He commanded us to preach to the people and to testify that He is the one whom God appointed as judge of the living and the dead. All the prophets testify about Him that everyone who believes in Him receives forgiveness of sins through His name."

Gunther raised his voice and said, "Repent of your sins and accept Jesus Christ as your Lord and Savior." Jakabee stood and watched as Gunther bowed his head. The people's hearts began to stir. Jakabee raised his hand and said, "If you want salvation you must pray and receive forgiveness of sins through Jesus Christ."

Much rejoicing was in Heaven that day.

I don't fully remember what happened next in the story, but I know that we received the God's Word every Sunday through the Parable Quest. My heart was so stirred by Pastor Rich's Parable Quest stories that I wanted my own quest. So, I made a commitment to God and went to college to study God's Word.

Now with a theology degree, I am ready to embark on my own quest with papers to pastor a small church not far from where I grew up, and the origination of the Parable Quest.

Gabe also wrote about his brother, John, in his next e-mail.

Chapter 3

Brother John's Parable Quest Remembrance

My younger brother, John, took a much different direction in his life, but was still serving God in the capacity that the Lord has instilled in him. John is shy and quiet, but has a deep love for God and loves to tell stories to children.

John got married a couple of years ago and his wife encouraged John to get his children's book published called *The Hidden Treasure*.

When I asked John what he remembered of the Parable Quest he told me of this one part that has stuck with him.

Jakabee and Gunther on the Parable Quest were invited to a large banquet in their honor. When they arrived, Jakabee wanted to sit at the head of the table, but Gunther had this to share with Jakabee:

Jesus told a parable of those who were invited to

a banquet. "He noticed that they chose the places of honor, and said to them, 'When you are invited by anyone to a feast, do not sit down in a place of honor, lest a more prominent man than you be invited by him; and he who invited you both will come and say to you,

'Give place to this man,' and you will be shamed, and told to take the lowest place.'

But when you are invited, go and sit in the lowest place, so that when your host comes he may say to you, 'Friend, go up higher;' then you will be honored in the presence of all who sit at the table with you. For everyone who exalts himself will be humbled, and he who humbles himself will be exalted.

He said also to the man who had invited him, 'When you give a dinner or a banquet, do not invite your friends or your brothers or your kinsmen or rich neighbors, lest they also invite you in return, and you be repaid.

When you give a feast, invite the poor, the maimed, the lame, the blind, and you will be blessed, because they cannot repay you. You will be repaid at the resurrection of the just.'"

Gunther made his way to a spot less prominent than the others, and Jakabee followed. When the man that held this banquet saw them he came in and escorted them to the head of the table.

"This was just as Jesus had said." Jakabee whispered.

John's children's book was inspired by one of the Parables of Jesus, and I've sent you a copy of it.

When I got home, I sat down with John's book in my most comfortable chair near my fireplace, turned off the TV and began to read.

A young girl went to the country to visit her grandmother and grandfather. The old farm was no longer used for farming as it had been in the past, but they still had some cows, chickens and a glorious garden not only with fruits and vegetables, but with wonderful bright flowers that make it seem like you are in another world surrounded by flowers of pinks, blues and reds.

Grandma and the young girl tended to the flowers

as Grandpa tended to the vegetables. At night Grandpa would read from his Bible to her, then he would tell her a story that he would make up or share from his past.

This night was different. She was now 10 years old and Grandpa was getting very old.

He began this story ever so softly, almost in a whisper, "My child, I am getting old, so I must tell you of the Colben Treasure. This treasure has been hidden for centuries, but I know where it is kept. I will tell you dear child if you promise to use it for good."

"Uh huh," the little girl said.

"Bring a piece of paper and one of your pencils and I will write down where you must go to find this treasure. You will not understand now, but on your 21st birthday this letter will be handed to you. It will be your choice to believe in the treasure or not, and it will be up to you to find it."

Grandpa told her the story of Fredrick Colben, a prince who was not the king's favorite. He was overlooked on many family occasions, because he had fifteen brothers and sisters. It was easy for

Fredrick to go unnoticed, because he often hid and was full of scheming mischief.

On Fredrick's 18th birthday, he devised a plan to take from his father the king's treasures and start his own life away from there. Fredrick and an accomplice missed the family weekend outing. He was again forgotten.

They hid themselves by the vault where the treasure was. They put the treasure in large jugs that would normally hold water, then took the two jugs and set out on their own adventure. But as with most larceny, it did not end on a happy note.

Young Fredrick found a large hole that had been dug for a well years ago, but now was abandoned. He put one of the jugs ever so carefully in the old well and then went back to the castle to fetch the other that his accomplice was watching until he returned. Fredrick found that his accomplice was gone and so was the other jug.

As he stood in bewilderment at being snookered, his family returned unannounced and there he was standing by the emptied vault. Fredrick had not known that one of the servants stayed behind and had seen the whole thing.

Fredrick's accomplice was soon found with the stolen goods. Fredrick and his so-called friend lost their heads that day. Only the servant who stayed behind knew of the other jug buried in the well. The servant never disclosed this information, because he feared the king. When the king had died and one of the sons took his place, the missing treasure was forgotten. The servant wrote a map to the treasure, so when his sons became old enough they could unbury the treasure and use it for good. His sons did not believe their father, because he told many stories, so the map remained a family -fable to this day.

Grandpa said that he was a descendant of this servant. He never searched for the treasure because he had all that he longed for with the farm, but had often wondered about the treasure and its map which he had kept all these years along with its story.

On her 21st birthday the girl remembered grandpa's story, but grandpa had been gone many years. In fact, he passed away a couple of years after he told her the story.

"I don't think the story or the letter will ever come to me," she thought. The next day as she was preparing to go to work at the real estate agency where she was a loan officer, she heard a knock at the door. This irritated her because she was already running late. *Who could this be?* she wondered.

She cracked the door open and peeked out and saw a man in a brown uniform holding a registered letter. "Who is it and what do you want?" "I have a certified letter addressed to a Cynthia Shields," he answered. She left the chain on the door and allowed him to hand the letter and clipboard through the door.

She signed the clipboard, took the letter and thanked the delivery man. It was from a lawyer in the town where grandpa and grandma lived. She opened the envelope and saw just what she hoped it to be: the story that grandpa told her about, with a map and everything.

Cindy's parents both had high paying jobs and were not interested in any wives tales or stories of treasures. Cindy had been pretty much on her own since she was 17. She lived with her grandparents, who loved her very much. When

Cindy was a child, her parents had plenty of money but not enough time for children. She began to get into trouble and failed to do her school work. While spending time with her grandparents, she saw something different in them. They spent a lot of time at church, and when Cindy would visit, she reluctantly went with them, but she always felt better for going.

At age 13 is when her grandparents took her in for good and she began to improve in school and attitude. Through their love and help she found she was good with numbers and loved real estate. Her grandmother was a real estate agent, so it just fit when she took some tests and learned about mortgage loans. At 19 years old she became one of the youngest loan processors the company ever had.

Now at 21 she had her own condo overlooking the ocean and a newer car. She went into the office with the letter and began to research the whereabouts of this mystery Prince Fredrick. *The letter describes what seems to be an English castle, but where?* she thought.

The internet gave some help on a story of a King Fredrick. She began to plan her trip to England.

From her research she found that Fredrick was from Ruthin Castle Denbighshire, North Wales.

The ancient remains of its castle are some of the oldest in Wales. It originated in 1277 by order of Edward I, years before the great fortresses of Conway and Caernarvon. Lynn Gruffield's brother, Danby, built a castle at Ruthin, but forfeited it when he rebelled with his brother Edward. Edward I's queen, Eleanor, was in residence in 1281, so it must have been habitable by then. Reginald de Grey, Justice of Chester and a marcher lord (marcher lords were strong, trusted lords appointed by the king to guard the borders of the king's territory) was entrusted with the defense of Ruthin in 1277. He completed the castle in 1284.

De Grey was given the borders of Defferncott territory for service to the king. His family occupied for the next 226 years as ruler, in effect, an English Hundred. In England, a "Hundred" was the division of a shire for administrative, military and judicial purposes under the common law.

In 1646, the castle survived an eleven week siege during the Civil War, but was demolished in 1648.

In 1677 Sir Thomas Middleton's brother, Richard, bought the property. When he died in 1796, the courts awarded his estates to his three daughters, and Maria received Ruthin Castle.

Maria moved to Ruthin in 1826 having married King Fredrick in 1798. This is where the story is lost on Prince Fredrick who was named after his father. No records were found of Prince Fredrick II.

Cindy made accommodations at the Manorhaus in Llangollen, Wales.

She flew into Liverpool, rented a car and drove to the inn. Having arrived early in the evening, she thought it best to get some food and head to bed early so she'd be ready for the quest that lay ahead.

The next morning was glorious as the rays from sunrise streamed into her room. She pulled out her grandpa's papers and carefully studied them. The old well that held the jug could be under a house now or could be anywhere.

She received directions to the Ruthin Castle and found everything she hoped for. The woods around the castle told her that there was a possibility that it had not been disturbed. She went into the castle and inquired about the vaults in which the king would have kept his most valuable items.

She was told that there were chambers in the lower part of the east wing of the castle where they figured the king would have kept his treasures. She was not allowed to go to the chambers but she did not need to.

Fredrick must have come out the east side of the castle somehow, she thought.

Rounding the outside of the castle, Cindy found a small opening from the east side that a person could easily walk through. Now that she had a good idea of the route that Fredrick took, she just needed to figure out where the well was.

More easily said than done. The courtyard went out of a large gate through the estate and then to the dense forest. It could be anywhere out in that forest. She gathered her thoughts and went back to the Wild Pheasant Hotel to eat and gather more information. Cindy now had only three days left of her so-called vacation to locate the jug in the well.

The forest is fenced off, so now what can I do? she thought. She decided to go back in the morning to talk with the castle curator, a tall distinguished man in his 70s.

Arriving bright and early, she began asking questions about Prince Fredrick and his beheading.

The curator knew about a beheading, but did not really know about the reason for it or who the victim was. Cindy explained to the curator that she was in search of an old well out from the eastside in the forest. She requested permission to go into the forest to locate this well. The curator looked at her like she was crazy. "I cannot allow you to wander out in these woods by yourself. Why would you need to find this well?"

"Well..." Cindy decided to tell the curator the truth, and explained the whole story to him. He laughed a little, but was sympathetic to her mission. He said he would help her find the well on Sunday because that was his day off.

On Sunday after a brief breakfast, Cindy headed

to the castle only to discover that the curator had not arrived. She was beginning to wonder if he would ever arrive, and just as her patience was wearing thin she saw a 1960s style, green MG coming up the road.

He apologized for his tardiness and mumbled something about having to first have his tea. The day was sunny and warm already and being somewhat before noon, had the potential to be a hot day. He told her of an old map inside the castle, which he hoped would shed light on where this well might be. He also said that if this treasure is real, then the officials would have to be brought in and a special team of archeologists would have to excavate the find.

She was not pleased with this thought because of the trouble she had been through, but she also knew that she would never be able to prove the story without help. Reluctantly she agreed, and they went in to inspect the map.

This map was very archaic. The castle was drawn out, but it did not show any of the countryside surrounding it. This map proved to be of no use, and she suggested venturing into the forest to look for it.

They approached the east corner of the grounds and proceeded past the fence into the dense forest. The curator had sense enough to bring a machete to cut some of the brush so they could get through.

This proved futile, because the brush was just too thick. After a few yards into it, the curator finally determined, "We cannot proceed this way," and turned back.

Climbing back over the fence and heading back to the castle, she felt all hope was lost, knowing she had to leave for home in two days. Cindy asked if there were any pictures or paintings done of the castle that they could inspect. The curator thought for a moment and named eight to ten pictures around the castle that could be potentially helpful.

The castle was closing, so there was no time to look that day. "But, what are you doing this evening?" He invited her over to his house to meet his wife of more than 40 years and have dinner. She gratefully accepted.

His home was a modest yet very quaint cottage, which was quite charming for an English gentleman and his wife. The home was on the outskirts of town on its own acreage.

As they pulled up in the MG, a lovely older woman came out of the house to greet them. She was petite with lovely long white hair, and she wore a colorful dress with an orchid print. The curator introduced his wife as Emily and he finally told her his name was William. Cindy also introduced herself. The conversation they had over dinner was quite pleasant, but not much was said about the treasure hunt.

William took her back to the Manorhaus and said, "Don't give up so easily. If you really believe what your grandfather told you then nothing should stop you from finding the treasure."

Wow, that is hard to hear. I'm all ready to pack and head back to the States and forget about this crazy notion of a treasure, she thought to herself.

While lying in bed that night she thought of her grandfather and all that he had said. Tears filled her eyes, and not just because she missed her grandparents, but also it felt like the search was becoming hopeless, especially since she continued to run into so many road blocks to the truth.

The next morning she felt refreshed for some reason, and made the decision to stay until she found the treasure, no matter how long it took. She made a phone call to inform her boss that she would be staying, and rather than letting her quit, they offered her a six-month leave of absence. Her own condo was to be put up for sale in order to finance her stay.

Now that's faith and commitment, she thought, as she headed to the castle to talk with William. William was waiting for her. Her eyes lit up as she saw all the equipment he had brought in to help get through the tough brush. She also noticed a young man dressed in a jumpsuit and work gloves.

William waved to her and she approached with great excitement and anticipation. The young man was introduced as Steven, a friend of the castle and a historian and archeologist. Cindy hugged William and said, "When can we start?' They first scanned the paintings in the castle and found one that had a well in it. This well seemed to be in the general direction of the east side, and very close to a large oak tree.

"This must be it!" she said eagerly. They

proceeded to the back of the east side and into the thick brush. The gas powered tools removed the brush, and quickly they made headway into the forest. Because of the thickness of the brush it was hard to see any large trees. Discouragement and bewilderment set in once again.

In almost happenstance, Cindy was exhausted and leaned against a large tree to rest. Steven stood in shock as did William. Cindy was clueless, until William smiled and said, "Cindy, you are leaning against the tree."

With a little more probing, to her left were signs of what could have been a well. Laughter and tears welled up in Cindy, and they returned back to the castle to get the proper digging equipment. Shovels and pick axes and small trowel shovels were used to carefully dig in the well. As Steven delicately moved the earth from the hole, Cindy and William helped by removing brush from around the area to give him more room. The digging went on endlessly, yet Steven seemed more determined with each scoop of earth he shoveled.

He hit something. They all heard the ping. The anticipation bubbled out of them. Now, ever so cautiously he used the trowel to move the dirt from around it. As he reached down to touch it, he found it to be only a rock. "Ugh, just a rock." He grabbed the rock and threw it aside, but to his astonishment he saw the top of a large jar. Their screams of excitement could have been heard for miles away. Steven dug around the jar until he could wiggle it loose, and out it came.

They did not want to empty the jar in the woods so they carried it like a precious baby back to the castle. Once inside, the top was carefully removed to reveal the most magnificent jewels that anyone had ever seen. Each one sparkled with brilliance like the noonday sun. There were an amazing assortment of colors, shapes and sizes of rings, necklaces, earrings, pendants, and individual jewels.

They lined them up on the floor of the room. The timeworn, yet finely crafted gold and silver settings made their hearts patter with excitement. They all stood there overwhelmed, and finally William said, "We must keep it all together intact, with the jar."

Steven and Cindy looked at each other, nodded and firmly agreed. Unbeknownst to Cindy,

William was not the curator of the castle. By birth, William was the heir; the owner of Ruthin Castle and its grounds.

"Much thanks to you, Cindy. Without the love and trust in your grandparents, unearthing our family treasure and heritage would have been impossible." William generously gave Cindy and Steven a share of the priceless treasure, although much of it was kept with the jar on display at the museum inside the castle.

Throughout the process, Cindy and Steven became good friends. Their friendship grew into love, and they were married in Liverpool, England, and explored most of Europe on their honeymoon. Cindy gave up everything to seek a treasure that she trusted was real. Her trust and faith in what she believed proved to be a great treasure in a jar.

We seek a greater treasure than what Cindy found, and it's worthy of giving up everything for.

The Bible says in the book of Matthew 13:44-46, "The kingdom of heaven is like treasure hidden in a field, which a man found and covered up; then in his joy he goes and sells all that he has and buys that field.

Again, the kingdom of heaven is like a merchant in search of fine pearls, who, on finding one pearl of great value, went and sold all that he had and bought it."

In a similar fashion, God offers us His kingdom. It is an incomparable treasure at a price we can never afford!

We can't pay the full price for the life which God gives us, but when we exchange our life for the life which God offers, we receive a treasure beyond compare. Discovering God's kingdom is like finding hidden treasure. When we discover the kingdom of God, we receive the greatest possible treasure: the Lord, Himself, is our highest, most precious treasure.

In this story, Cindy finds her hidden treasure, but for us it refers to the Kingdom of God. The Lord, Himself, is the treasure we seek. If the Almighty is your gold and your precious silver, then you will delight yourself in the Almighty (Job 22:22-23).

Is the Lord the treasure and delight of your heart? John prayed, "Lord Jesus, reveal to us the true riches of Your kingdom. Help us to set our hearts on You alone as the treasure beyond compare.

Free our hearts of any desires or attachments, so that we may freely give to You all that we have in joy and gratitude for all that You have given to us. May we always find joy and delight in your presence. And all the children said, "Amen."

I closed John's book and re-read Gabe's most recent email.

I am very proud of my brother, John, for his commitment and love for God and family. You mentioned you are also looking for Bill Simpson. I have found an article that was written about him that might help.

God's Grace be with you.
Sincerely,
Gabe Smith.

His e-mail ended with that, and I shut down my computer for the evening.

Wow! I thought as I pondered what I had just read. *David, Gabe and John are all following the Lord and making reference to the Parable Quest.*

Chapter 4

The Heart of Praise

Even as a youth, Bill had always been very talented at music. He could play just about any instrument he picked up.

When I typed his name into a search engine, I found this article on a Christian music review website. It looks like his mom had posted this story about Bill:

Bill was very talented, but it was his love for God that drove him to increase his musical skills. As a young man he could play many kinds of instruments and was also a gifted painter. He won numerous awards and contests in high school and proceeded on to college to study arts and music. Becoming a music pastor had been his goal, and when it was reached, this work became the greatest joy for him; greater than all the riches that this world has to offer.

A few months ago Bill was called into his senior pastor's office where he learned that the new senior pastor wanted his son to lead worship, and they would have to terminate Bill's employment there. Bill fell on his knees because of the hurt he felt by this decision, but he got up, shook the pastor's hand and walked away.

His severance package wasn't much, and he would need to find new work as soon as possible.

Bill called his best friend, Gabe, whom he has known since his Sunday School days, and told him of his difficult situation. Gabe prayed with him over the phone, and they met for lunch at a coffee shop close by a couple days later.

As they talked, a man sitting overheard their conversation and came up and apologized for eavesdropping. He was a pastor and asked Bill to come and see him tomorrow at 9 am, then handed him his card and walked out.

Bill read the card: "New Hope Church, Senior Pastor Mark Anderson."

"That is fitting," Bill said to Gabe, "for God is good and He shows Himself faithful."

The next day Bill met with Pastor Mark and they

prayed, and both felt good about Bill coming on staff as their Music Pastor. Pastor Mark said he had been praying for a music pastor with a heart for ministry, and he did not expect to have it answered at a coffee shop while eavesdropping on someone's conversation!

The music pastor position that Pastor Mark offered Bill turned out to be better financially and closer to his home. Bill prayed as they ended the interview, "Thank you, Father God, for Your provision and bringing us together to do Your will." Pastor Mark added, "Amen." Later that evening, while contemplating God's plans and purposes, Bill remembered the Parable Quest from his school days, and shared one of the teachings with Pastor Mark in an email.

> *Jakabee and Gunther had just completed a meeting with the townspeople, when Gunther shared these parting stories:*
>
> *"A nobleman went into a far country to receive a kingdom and then returned. Calling ten of his servants, he gave them $10,000, and said to them, 'Trade with these until I come.'*
>
> *But his citizens hated him and sent an embassy*

after him, saying, 'We do not want this man to reign over us.' When he returned, having received the kingdom, he commanded these servants, to whom he had given the money, to be called to him, that he might know what they had gained by trading.

The first came before him, saying, 'Lord, your $10,000 has made $10,000 more.' And he said to him, 'Well done, good servant! Because you have been faithful in a very little, you shall have authority over ten cities.'

And the second came, saying, 'Lord, your $10,000 has made $5000.' And he said to him, 'And you are to be over five cities.' Then another came, saying, 'Lord, here is your $1000, which I kept laid away in a napkin; for I was afraid of you, because you are a severe man; you take up what you did not lay down, and reap what you did not sow.'

The nobleman said to him, 'I will condemn you out of your own mouth, you wicked servant!

You knew that I was a severe man, taking up what I did not lay down and reaping what I did not sow? Why then did you not put my money into the bank, and at my coming I should have collected it with interest?'

And he said to those who stood by, 'Take the $1000 from him, and give it to him who has the $10,000.' (And they said to him, 'Lord, he has $10,000!') 'I tell you, that to everyone who has will be given more; but from him who has not, even what he has will be taken away. But as for these enemies of mine, who did not want me to reign over them, bring them here and slay them before me.'"

"For the kingdom of heaven is like a householder who went out early in the morning to hire laborers for his vineyard. After agreeing with the laborers for an amount of money a day, he sent them into his vineyard. And going out again the third hour he saw others standing idle in the marketplace; and to them he said, 'You go into the vineyard too, and whatever is right I will give you.' So they went.

Going out again about the sixth hour and the ninth hour, he did the same. And about the eleventh hour he went out and found others standing; and he said to them, 'Why do you stand here idle all day?'

They said to him, 'Because no one has hired us.' He said to them, 'You go into the vineyard too.'

And when evening came, the owner of the vineyard said to his steward, 'Call the laborers and pay them their wages, beginning with the last, up to the first.'

When those hired about the eleventh hour came, each of them received the same amount. Now when the first came, they thought they would receive more; but each of them also received the same amount.

And on receiving it they grumbled at the householder, saying, 'These last worked only one hour, and you have made them equal to us who have borne the burden of the day and the scorching heat.'

But he replied to one of them, 'Friend, I am doing you no wrong; did you not agree with me for an amount of money? Take what belongs to you, and go; I choose to give to this last as I give to you. Am I not allowed to do what I choose with what belongs to me? Or do you begrudge my generosity?'

So the last will be first, and the first last."

Gunther said to Jakabee, "Let us also remember that the gifts, and talents that we have are from God, to invest in others where rust and moths can't steal our treasures."

Here ends the stories I collected from my Sunday School friends about the Parable Quest. Now I need to put them into a book to share with friends and family, if not the whole world.

CHAPTER 5

Chapter 5

The Eulogy

"Richard 'Rich' Norton Jr. died of coronary complications at Emmanuel Hospital. He was born in Seattle, to Richard and Tammy Norton. Rich was a senior pastor at Hope Life Church, and then a youth pastor of Community Fellowship Church. Rich is survived by his wife Jennifer, the students he ministered to and the congregation he served. He passed away peacefully, surrounded by family and friends. He will be greatly missed, yet we know he is being told by God, "Well done good and faithful servant. Enter into your rest."

The local paper carried this obituary of my pastor and friend.

At the Eulogy, I walked in and knew the others who had been in the Sunday School class with me wouldn't recognize me.

While walking by a side room, I heard several men sharing about the adventures of the Parable Quest, except they mentioned they were missing someone named Jonathan. No one seemed too shocked. From their conversation, I gleaned that they saw him as someone who would listen when he came to church, but always seemed distant from the rest of the group.

Hmmm, this is going to be a surprise, I thought, as the corner of my mouth formed a soft smile.

I listened a while longer near the doorway. Each man began to share their story of how Pastor Rich had impacted their lives. Pastor Rich and his wife had no children of their own, but he had always called them his kids.

Unfortunately, the busyness of life had kept them from keeping in contact with their mentor and pastor as they grew older. Gabe told how he was probably the last to see and talk with Pastor Rich, because Rich had attended his college graduation a few years ago.

Pastor Rich would have been so happy with how all his boys had grown in the Lord. "What about Jonathan?" David asked. "We need to contact him somehow." All the boys were there, David Broz, brothers John and Gabe Smith and Bill Simpson, but no Jonathan Breen.

In the back of the room, unbeknownst to them, I, Jonathan Breen, stood in silence as each one came and sat down. Whispers flooded the room about *who was doing the eulogy?* A tall man stood up from the second row and moved to the front.

"Thank you for coming today. We are going to start in just a few minutes, please take your seats." I stepped past the tall man and approached the front of the sanctuary. I reached for the mic as I had done many times before in my profession as a Christian talk-radio DJ.

I introduced myself, "Hello friends and family. It's good to see you all here to celebrate the life of Pastor Rich Norton. I'm JT of Christian Talk Radio KRYS, also known to most of you as Jonathan T. Breen. Pastor Rich was my youth pastor in 5th through 10th grade, then my family moved to the big city because of my father's job."

As I surveyed the crowd once they knew it was me, I saw a few gaping mouths and stunned looks on several faces. I continued, "Many of you can remember the impact of Pastor Rich's stories, the Parable Quest, had on the youth.

These stories have had remarkable effect on me,

and from what I hear, have had the same effect many of you as well. I would like to take these next moments and allow the others from my class to come and share about Pastor Rich."

Each one stepped forward shocked to see me there, and amazed most of all to know that I, too, was actually serving the Lord.

After they shared, I came back to the mic and talked about the one Parable Quest story that most profoundly affected my life.

Jakabee and Gunther were on their journey, as a young man quickly walked past them mumbling to himself. They could not help but take notice of him, because of the stench that clouded about him.

They caught up with him enough to communicate, but downwind enough to breathe fresh air. Jakabee asked, "Where are you going in such a hurry?"

Gunther secretly hoped the young man was going somewhere to take a shower.

The young man stopped, shoulders drooping

and arms hanging down in defeat, and began to sob as he told his story of how he had used his money to live the fun life of partying. All the friends he had made laughed at him and threw him in the mud when the money was gone. He was able to get work tending pigs, hence the smell, and now decided to go home to his dad and ask to work for him. His dad's hired hands got more money than he did tending pigs.

"Do you think your dad will take you back smelling like this, and because you wasted his money?" asked Gunther.

The young man stopped crying and smiled and said, "My dad is very good to all who work for him, and he has always been good to me."

"I love my dad," he continued on, "and I know my dad loves me."

"How far is your dad's home," Jakabee asked.

"Not much farther," the young man replied.

As Jakabee and Gunther continued to walk with the disheveled man up a dusty road, an old man approached from the other direction wearing marvelous clothes fit for a king. The old man ran towards us, and embraced the young man. The young man tried to speak to his father, but was silenced by the tears and love that the father had for him.

The old man yelled for the servant to prepare a feast, because his son was home, alive. However the young man's older brother was angry and said to his father, "Why should my brother receive so much since he wasted everything you gave him?"

The dad smiled and said, "Everything I have shall be yours my son, but your brother was dead and now is alive and back home, so you also should be glad."

Gunther opened his Bible and read a story Jesus told. He said, "A certain man had two sons. The younger of them said to his father, 'Father, give me my share of your property.' He divided his livelihood between them.

Not many days after, the younger son gathered all of this together and traveled into a far country. There he wasted his property with riotous living. When he had spent all of it, there arose a severe famine in that country and he began to be in need. He went and joined himself to one of the citizens of that country, and he sent him into his fields to feed pigs.

He wanted to fill his belly with the husks that the pigs ate, but no one gave him any. But when he came to himself he said, 'How many hired servants of my fathers have bread enough to spare, and I'm dying with hunger!

I will get up and go to my father, and will tell him, 'Father, I have sinned against heaven, and in your sight. I am no more worthy to be called your son. Make me as one of your hired servants."

He arose, and came to his father. But while he was still far off, his father saw him, and was moved with compassion, and ran, and fell on his neck, and kissed him. The son said to him, 'Father, I have sinned against heaven, and in your sight. I am no longer worthy to be called your son.' But the father said to his servants, 'Bring out the best robe, and put it on him. Put a ring on his hand, and shoes on his feet. Bring the fattened calf, kill it, and let us eat, and celebrate; for this, my son, was dead, and is alive again. He was lost, and is found.' They began to celebrate. Now his elder son was in the field. As he came near to the house, he heard music and dancing. He called one of the servants to him, and asked what was going on.

The servant said to him, 'Your brother has come, and your father has killed the fattened calf, because he has received him back safe and healthy.'

But the elder son was angry, and would not go in. Therefore his father came out, and begged him. But he answered his father, 'Behold, these many years I have served you, and I never disobeyed a commandment of yours, but you never gave me a goat that I might celebrate with my friends. But when this, your son, came, who has devoured your living with prostitutes, you killed the fattened calf for him.'

He said to him, 'Son, you are always with me, and all that is mine is yours. But it was appropriate to celebrate and be glad, for this, your brother, was dead, and is alive again. He was lost, and is found.'"

Gunther smiled and said, "God loves even the

lost sinner who turns around, and heads back to Him, and God rewards those who diligently seek Him."

I, myself, was a prodigal son of sorts. Yes, it was true I didn't want to listen to the stories of the Parable Quest, but each week I could hardly wait to hear what would happen next.

When we moved, I found new friends and lots of trouble, but prior to graduating from college, I received a phone call one evening from Pastor Rich. He reminded me of the Parable I just mentioned, and that it was not too late. He encouraged me to give up vain pursuits, and to serve and love God. I changed my business major shortly after and transferred to a small Bible college, received a Bachelor's degree in communications, and started with a small radio station as an understudy.

Soon I was doing some announcements and then trusted with my own radio program, and the rest is history. I told the guys from the old youth group to share what they remembered of the Parable Quest today, so I could put it in a book for all of us. Many stories were shared by Pastor Rich, and I have done my best to document all that I remembered of what was said.

After speaking from my heart, I then gave a tender message ending with an opportunity for those who had not accepted Jesus Christ as their personal Savior to raise their hands and allow us to pray for them just as Pastor Rich would have done.

Chapter 6

Background of Pastor Rich, by Mrs. Norton

Pastor Rich's widow, Mrs. Jennifer Norton, shared some of their life stories for me to add to the works put into the book, *The Parable Quest*.

It was a hot July evening at Brown Lake Bible Camp, and a young youth pastor was excited to minister to the youth he had been entrusted with at Christ Fellowship Church.

The rookie pastor's name was Rich Norton, a tall, thin rugged man. At just 22 years old he had recently finished his Bachelor's degree in Theology and was working on his Masters. Rich grew up with a family that went to a little Baptist church. After being led to Christ by the youth pastor in that country church, he knew without a doubt that he wanted to become a youth pastor someday.

A friend invited him to a youth rally on praying for the lost, and at that rally he met his soon-to-be wife, Jennifer. Jennifer was a short, thin, bubbly, blue-eyed brunette, and had a real call from the Lord to minister to youth as well.

They married in his second year of his Master's program, and they began to lead a team to reach out to the youth in the community with after-school programs. The ministry was very stressful for this new couple, but also fruitful as youth began to come to Christ Jesus.

A fellow student invited him to an outreach event at his Foursquare Church and Rich and Jennifer went. Little did they know that this would be the beginning of a confirmation of their ministry. As the congregation began to sing and pray in tongues, Rich began to confess his sins to the Lord, and asked God if he could also have what these people were experiencing.

He looked over at Jennifer who had her eyes closed, tears steadily streaming down her cheek. Rich's mind wandered and lost track of what the pastor was talking about, but saw people coming forward for prayer. Jennifer looked over at Rich with a smile and said, "Let's go forward," as she took his hand.

They got up and walked towards the front, but Rich still did not know what the pastor had called people forward for. Waiting at the end of the prayer line, the two stood watching as the pastor prayed for each person. The Spirit of God fell on all of them and ministered to them while they laid on the floor. Rich being from a church not accustomed to this kind of *God ministering* felt a little uneasy, but excited as the pastor advanced closer to Jennifer and himself.

It was their turn. The pastor stood in front of them and asked how he could pray for them. Rich blurted out, "We want a fresh anointing of the Holy Spirit and to fulfill our ministry." Jennifer looked at Rich with surprise and excitement, her cute little grin radiating.

The pastor laid his hand on both of their shoulders and he began to pray: "Dear Heavenly Father, as this young couple has requested, may they receive all that is in their hearts and may they receive a fresh anointing in the ministry you have called them to."

Rich and Jennifer held each other in a loving embrace as they cried in the presence of God's love as He confirmed their ministry.

Rich finished his master's degree, and at 30 years old he and Jennifer were given a pastorate of a large church where the former pastor had to step down. Rich grew restless knowing that God was calling him somewhere else. But where? Now after seven years, the church had grown to well over 2,000 members and Rich's staff had grown as well. Even so, he couldn't shake the feeling of missing what God had for him.

Jennifer came home one day from the store telling Rich about a woman she ran into in the frozen food section (almost literally), and as they talked the woman began to cry. She shared about how their church longed for a youth pastor, but no one would come because the town was small. It had only 100 people and just a handful of youth.

This woman explained how every year she would see the kids stop coming to church and end up in trouble – every single one of them. Jennifer was deeply moved but thought *Rich would definitely not want to move away from his thriving ministry.*

Rich looked at Jennifer, smiled and said, "What do you think about us taking that position?" She replied, "We would need to get regular jobs to support ourselves, but it would be a real opportunity to serve the Lord beyond ourselves."

"A major step of faith," Jennifer added with a smile of her own. "And who would take over the youth ministry we have now?"

There were many questions, but Rich and Jennifer knew what to do. They got on their knees and talked to God.

A meeting with the pastoral staff was arranged and they talked with a few friends about it for their prayer support. The meeting with the pastors went well, and Rich recommended that a couple who had been on staff with the youth for over four years become the new pastors. This couple showed great ability to teach and lead well. The staff would take this recommendation under advisement as Rich and Jennifer submitted their resignations.

While Rich and Jennifer walked home, a calming peace fell over them along with a great joy, as they knew they had made the right decision.

The pastor in the small town was overjoyed to meet them at Community Fellowship Church.

Pastor Jon Sterling was his name. He was a stout, balding man in his 60's with a genuine, welcoming smile. Judy, his wife was quite the opposite of him. She was tall and outgoing with a wonderful gift of hospitality.

Rich and Jennifer shared some of the needs and concerns they had in order to move and take this position. They also needed to find work. "Jon, do you know anyone looking for employees?" Jon looked up and stood, thinking, and then smiled. "Why yes, there is someone who could use your help, and maybe Jennifer could talk with Judy. She is on the school board and I know we need teachers. Rich, come with me. I want you to meet someone."

Rich was introduced to another pastor who happened to own a large farm with cattle and plantings of lentil and canola. Big Tim McCammer had the largest farm in the state and could always use help even from a green city slicker like Rich.

The arrangements were setup, and the following week Rich and Jennifer started their new life out on the farm. Rich and Jennifer moved into a little two bedroom, one bath home near the church on

Saturday and on Sunday were introduced to the congregation.

Big Tim's wife was Lucy. Amazingly, she was the woman Jennifer had run into at the store. Everyone was delighted to meet them, and they were introduced to the seven youth at the church: five boys and three girls.

The boy's names were David, Gabe, John, Bill, and Jonathan.

Rich began to teach them each week, but they seemed uninterested. So one night while he and Jennifer were praying and he was going through the Parables of Jesus, a story began in his head. The idea for the Parable Quest was born, and the next week he began teaching with it.

This background story by Mrs. Norton (Jennifer) brings the Parable Quest full circle. I told the guys I would put the memories into a book for them to hold on to and share with their families and friends. After all this writing, nothing was more profound than to think we never took the opportunity to tell this faithful Sunday School pastor about the impact he made on our lives and that the Parable Quest continues.

When you see a Sunday School teacher, please remember to thank them for their service in ministry.

Discussion Guide

Chapter 1:

David and Tom were in another country on a mission trip. What has been your experience with missions, reaching the lost for Jesus Christ?

Think about the Parable of "The Sower." How does the sower of seed fit in your life, and are you ready to produce?

Consider the Parable of the Good Samaritan. How have you been a Good Samaritan to others?

Have you experienced God's Holy Spirit and His loving presence like David and Tom?

Gunther and Jackabee used many Parables as they ministered and traveled. How has their story spoken to your life?

Chapter 2:

Gabe had a calling in his life to be a pastor, and he went for it. What is your calling? And how are you going for it? What steps can you take today towards it?

Gabe said, "I remembered wanting to be the one sown on good soil, a person who understands God's Word and is fruitful in his life." How are you being fruitful in your life?

Gunther raised his voice and said, "Repent of your sins and accept Jesus Christ as your Lord and Savior." What does repentance mean?

Chapter 3:

What was the Parable about a table that Gunther shared with Jakabee, and how does this have meaning to you?

What does the Bible say in the book of Matthew 13:44-46?

Is the Lord the treasure and delight of your heart?

Where is this verse found in the Bible, and how is the Lord your treasure and delight?

The kingdom of heaven is like a merchant in search of fine pearls. Where is this Parable found, and who represents the fine pearls?

Chapter 4:

Bill was very talented and could have used those talents any way he wanted to. What did he decide to do?

Look up the Parable of the Talents in your Bible. What are your talents?

What is your reaction when someone wrongs you, even in ministry?

How was Bill's reaction to being fired, honorable?

What scripture verses come to mind that encourage you to respond honorably when you are wronged?

Chapter 5:

Has a Sunday School teacher touched your life? In what way?

How are you touching others with the truth of Jesus Christ and His Great Commission?

The prodigal son had done many wrong things. What was his reason for returning?

When you are away from God, what is your reason for returning to Christ Jesus?

In the story of the prodigal, how have you been like the older son who stayed true to his father?

How was the older son rewarded?

What are the gifts the Father gives us?

Chapter 6:

How did the widow's story, Mrs. Norton, minister to you?

How did Rich and Jennifer receive leading of the Holy Spirit as they were sent out by the church? What has the Holy Spirit shown you?

How will you get involved with others in order to grow and share?

When did Rich and Jennifer step out in faith and do what God told them? What is God saying to you?

About the Author

Rick Overholtzer is more known to be behind or in front of the camera for his local TV show called "The Uncle Rick Show," which can be seen on YouTube.

He enjoys spending time with family and friends, and he could not have accomplished this book without their support.

He hopes that this story will inspire those that read it to enjoy God's Word and grow in their relationship with Jesus Christ.

The Parable Quest is proudly published by:

Creative Force Press

www.CreativeForcePress.com

Do You Have a Book in You?

www.ingramcontent.com/pod-product-compliance
Lightning Source LLC
Chambersburg PA
CBHW020010050426
42450CB00005B/393